JOIN,
or
DIE.

★★★★★★★★★★★★★

An American Patriot's Book of Quotes

JOIN, or DIE.

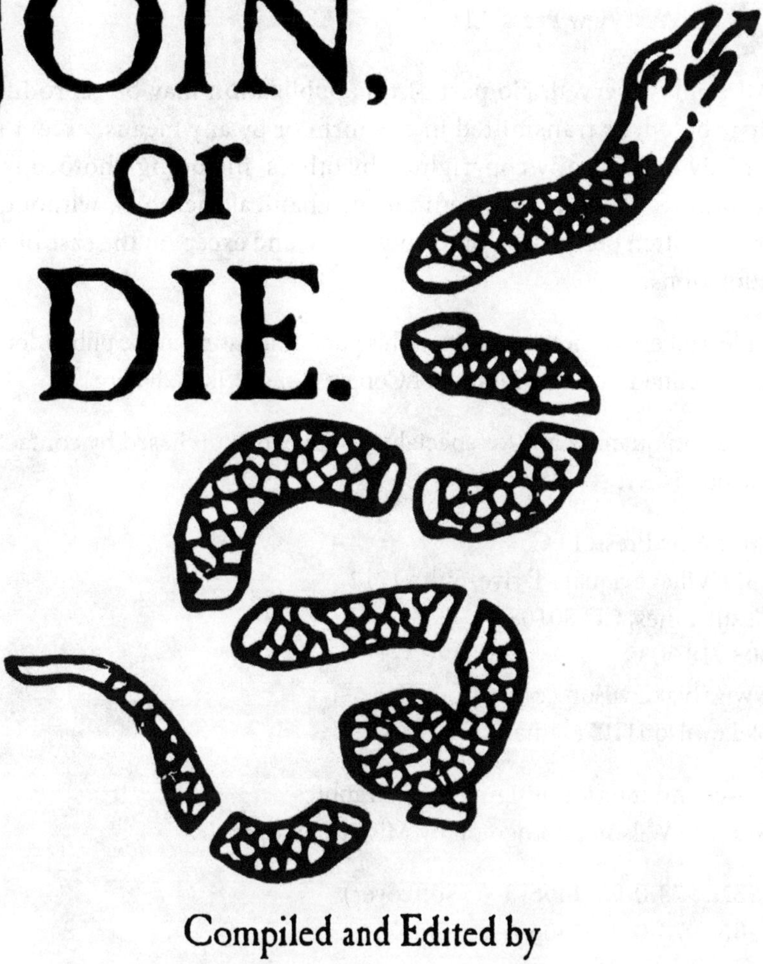

Compiled and Edited by

R. Blake Wilson

WestView Press, LLC

JOIN, or DIE. An American Patriot's Book of Quotes
Compiled and Edited by R. Blake Wilson

Published by

WestView Press, LLC

Books, in quantity and/or special sales, may be purchased by contacting the publisher:

WestView Press, LLC
7311 Village Square Drive, Suite 1712
Castle Pines, CO 80108
303 718 3039
www.rblakewilson.com
blakewilson1107@gmail.com

Cover and interior design by NZ Graphics
R. Blake Wilson photograph by Misha Photography

ISBN: 978-0-9831406-3-4 (Softcover)
ISBN: 978-0-9831406-4-1 (eBook)

Library of Congress Control Number: 2022905189

First Edition

Printed in the United States of America

★ For the American Patriot ★

This book is dedicated to
Colonel Clifton P. Schroeder, USMC, Retired
My friend, mentor, and American Patriot

And my children
Philip John and Anna Marie

May they live in an America where Freedom and Individual Liberty is abundant and prospers for Eternity.

May God Bless America !!!

CONTENTS

INTRODUCTION

JOIN, or DIE. - An American Patriot's Book of Quotes is my second book and a renewed reminder to all American Patriots that the battle between LIBERTY and TYRANNY in America continues.

Ten years ago, my first book, *DON'T TREAD ON ME - An American Patriot's Book of Quotes* was my way of spreading the American message of LIBERTY and my stand against TYRANNY. Today, my message is even more urgent. Americans must UNITE AS ONE NATION and JOIN TOGETHER to SAVE AMERICA !! We must NOT commit suicide from within as President Lincoln warned against:

"America will never be destroyed from the outside. If we falter and lose our freedoms, it will be because we destroyed ourselves."
- Abraham Lincoln

Today, America is under attack by the Marxist, Leftist, Socialist, Communist, Green Party and Progressive agenda which is promoted by a compliant Leftist News/Media, Globalists and the Democratic Party. The current U.S. President and Congress (March 2022) are submissive to, if not activists for, the Progressive Left. The WOKE agenda, defund the police movement, cancel culture, COVID mandates, massive government spending and resulting inflation, the destruction and dismantling of the American energy sector, the open borders policy and elimination of border security, the BIG TECH agenda (which cancels President Trump yet allows access for Putin/Xi Jinping), the disastrous and embarrassing Biden Administration's Afghanistan withdrawal and, I will with caution add, the bought, rigged, and corrupt 2020 presidential election, and the January 6th Commission sham.... ALL have, by design, dangerously Divided and Weakened AMERICA and Diminished the AMERICAN CITIZEN's FREEDOM and LIBERTY.

"Single acts of tyranny may be ascribed to the accidental opinion of the day; but a series of oppressions, begun at a distinguished period, and pursued unalterably through every change of administration too plainly proves a deliberate, systemic plan of reducing us to slavery." - Thomas Jefferson

Our American Weakness and Divide has not only hurt America but also encouraged and emboldened the Enemies of Freedom throughout the world. American Strength and Leadership is critical.

Putin/Russia invaded Ukraine last month. Ali Khamenei/Iran continues to threaten Israel and America and build his/its nuclear program. Kim Jong-un/North Korea continues to expand and build his/its nuclear arsenal. And likely most threatening to LIBERTY and FREEDOM, Xi Jinping/China is rapidly growing his/its influence in the world and is building a military to rival America's strength with Taiwan as his/its first target. American Weakness and Division is a danger to LIBERTY and FREEDOM worldwide.

"It was leadership here at home that gave us strong American influence abroad, and the collapse of Imperial Communism. Great nations have responsibilities to lead, and we should always be cautious of those who would lower our profile, because they might just wind up lowering our flag." - Ronald Reagan.

Forever/Dictator Leaders who control these governments lead by Oppression and Tyranny over the individual citizen. INDIVIDUAL

★ INTRODUCTION ★

FREEDOM & LIBERTY is a natural God-given human trait and the desire of ALL Mankind. Americans must remember that we UNITED AS A NATION in 1776 to gain our LIBERTY & FREEDOM against Tyranny. The Founders of America created a perfect Republic and a perfect Constitution and Bill of Rights to secure our LIBERTY for eternity as long as we protect it with ALL our courage, strength and wisdom. Our freedoms are not guaranteed from generation to generation. Americans must JOIN TOGETHER as ONE NATION and demonstrate to the world that Government, of the people, by the people, for the people, shall not perish from this Earth!! We must UNITE AS AMERICANS!! We must JOIN, or DIE!!

"The people are the only sure reliance for the
PRESERVATION of our LIBERTY!"
- Thomas Jefferson

This book is a collection of quotes that I believe will inspire each reader, The American Patriot, to UNITE in the battle against Tyranny. UNITED WE STAND, DIVIDED WE FALL!!

May God Bless America !!

A Patriot's History Lesson

JOIN, or DIE.

JOIN, or DIE. is a political emblem attributed to Benjamin Franklin. The original publication by *The Pennsylvania Gazette* on May 9, 1754, is the earliest known political representation of colonial UNITY produced by an American colonist in Colonial America. Each cut segment of the snake represents a British colony in early America. Franklin's goal was to unite the colonists to combat the French and their Native American allies, and to support a unified colonial government in America. In the Revolutionary War, colonists used this image as a symbol of unity against the British rule. Today, this image is used as an American patriotic symbol of UNITY against TYRANNY.

The American Flag

American Flag 2022

The current design of the U.S. flag is its 27th; the design of the flag has been modified officially 26 times since 1777. The 48-star flag was in effect for 47 years until the 49-star version became official on July 4, 1959. The 50-star flag was ordered by then president Eisenhower on August 21, 1959, and was adopted on July 1960. It is the longest-used version of the U.S. flag and has been in use for over 61 years. The 50 stars on the flag represent the 50 U.S. states, and the 13 stripes represent the thirteen British colonies that declared independence from the Kingdom of Great Britain, and became the first states in the United States.

Nicknames for the flag include the Stars and Stripes, Old Glory, and the Star-Spangled Banner.

The Pledge of Allegience

American Flag 1892

"I pledge allegiance to my Flag and the Republic for which it stands, one nation, indivisible, with liberty and justice for all"
-1892 Captain George Thatcher Balch
Union Army Officer Civil War

"I pledge allegiance to the Flag of the United States of America, and to the Republic for which it stands, one Nation under God, indivisible, with liberty and justice for all."
- US Congress / Flag Day June 14th 1954

"In God We Trust"

The official motto of the United States.
It was adopted by the U.S. Congress in 1956,
replacing E Pluribus Unum (Out of Many, One),
which had been the de facto motto
since the initial 1776 design
on the Great Seal of the United States.

The Great Seal of the United States

The Great Seal of the United States is the symbol of our sovereignty as a nation. Its obverse is used on official documents to authenticate the signature of the President and it appears on proclamations, warrants, treaties, and commissions of high officials of the government. The Great Seal's design, used as our national coat of arms, is also used officially as decoration on the military uniform buttons, on plaques above the entrances to U.S. embassies and consulates, and in other places. Both the obverse and the less familiar reverse, which is never used as a seal, are imprinted on the one-dollar bill.

The history of the Great Seal begins with the founding of our nation. The Continental Congress appointed a committee to design a seal for the United States on July 4, 1776, just a few hours after they adopted the Declaration of Independence.

Description of Thompson's preliminary design for the Great Seal of the United States

On a field, Chevrons composed of seven pieces on one side and six on the other, joined together at the top in such wise that each of the six bears against or is supported by and supports two of the opposite side the pieces of the chevrons on each side alternate red & white. The shield borne on the breast of an American Eagle on the wing and rising proper. In the dexter talon of the Eagle an Olive branch & in the sinister a bundle of Arrows. Over the head of the Eagle a Constellation of Stars surrounded with bright rays and at a little distance clouds. In the bill of the Eagle a scroll with the words …

E PLURIBUS UNUM.

– Charles Thompson

United States President Oath of Office

I do solemnly swear that I will faithfully execute the Office of the President of the United States, and will to the best of my Ability, preserve, protect and defend the Constitution of the United States.
. . . So help me God.

– Article II, Section 1, Clause 8 United States Constitution

United States Congress
Oath of Office

I do solemnly swear that I will support and defend the Constitution of the United States against all enemies, foreign and domestic; that I will bear true faith and allegiance to the same; that I take this obligation freely, without any mental reservation or purpose of evasion; and that I will well and faithfully discharge the duties of the office on which I am about to enter.
... So help me God.

– Article VI, Clause 3 United States Constitution

Supreme Court of the United States Oath of Office

Justices of the Supreme Court of the United States are required to take two oaths before they may execute the duties of their appointed office.

The Constitutional Oath

I do solemnly swear that I will support and defend the Constitution of the United States against all enemies, foreign and domestic; that I will bear true faith and allegiance to the same; that I take this obligation freely, without any mental reservation or purpose of evasion; and that I will well and faithfully discharge the duties of the office on which I am about to enter.
. . . So help me God.

– Article VI, United States Constitution

The Judicial Oath

I do solemnly swear that I will administer justice without respect to persons, and do equal right to the poor and to the rich, and that I will faithfully and impartially discharge and perform all the duties incumbent upon me as under the Constitution and laws of the united States.

– Judiciary Act of 1789

"EQUAL JUSTICE UNDER LAW"

Declaration of Independence
July 4, 1776

Signing the Declaration of Independence.
Painting by John Trumbull, 1819

Here is the complete text of the Declaration of Independence. The original spelling and capitalization have been retained.

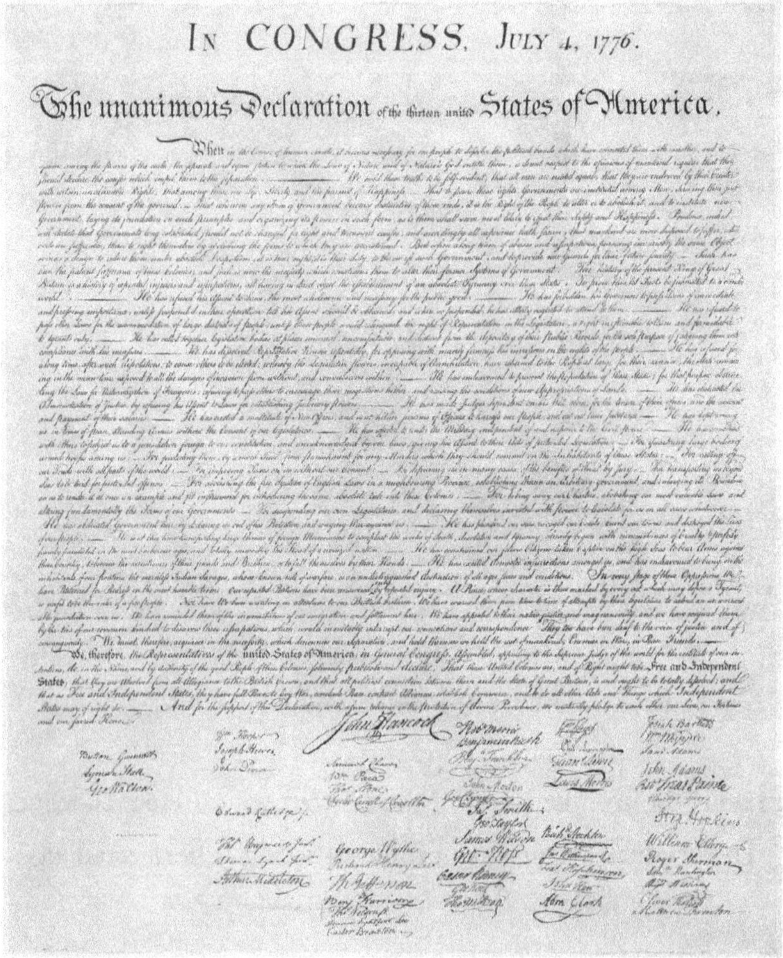

IN CONGRESS, JULY 4, 1776.

The unanimous Declaration of the thirteen united States of America,

Declaration of Independence

A DECLARATION BY THE REPRESENTATIVES OF THE UNITED STATES OF AMERICA, IN GENERAL CONGRESSS ASSEMBLED.

In Congress, July 4, 1776

The unanimous Declaration of the thirteen united States of America, When in the Course of human events, it becomes necessary for one people to dissolve the political bands which have connected them with another, and to assume among the powers of the earth, the separate and equal station to which the Laws of Nature and of Nature's God entitle them, a decent respect to the opinions of mankind requires that they should declare the causes which impel them to the separation.

We hold these truths to be self-evident, that all men are created equal, that they are endowed by their Creator with certain unalienable Rights, that among these are Life, Liberty and the pursuit of Happiness. That to secure these rights, Governments are instituted among Men, deriving their just powers from the consent of the governed, That whenever any Form of Government becomes destructive of these ends, it is the Right of the People to alter or to abolish it, and to institute new Government, laying its foundation on such principles and organizing its powers in such form, as to them shall seem most likely to effect their Safety and Happiness.

Prudence, indeed, will dictate that Governments long established should not be changed for light and transient causes; and accordingly all experience hath shewn, that mankind are more disposed to suffer, while evils are sufferable, than to right themselves by abolishing the forms to which they are accustomed. But when a long train of abuses and usurpations, pursuing invariably the same Object evinces a design to reduce them under absolute Despotism, it is their right, it is their duty, to throw off such Government, and to provide new Guards for their future security. Such has been the patient sufferance of these Colonies; and such is now the necessity which constrains them to alter their former Systems of Government. The history of the present King of Great Britain is a history of repeated injuries and usurpations, all having in direct object the establishment of an absolute Tyranny over these States. To prove this, let Facts be submitted to a candid world.

He has refused his Assent to Laws, the most wholesome and necessary for the public good.

He has forbidden his Governors to pass Laws of immediate and pressing importance, unless suspended in their operation till his Assent should be obtained; and when so suspended, he has utterly neglected to attend to them.

He has refused to pass other Laws for the accommodation of large districts of people, unless those people would relinquish the right of Representation in the Legislature, a right inestimable to them and formidable to tyrants only.

He has called together legislative bodies at places unusual, uncomfortable, and distant from the depository of their public Records, for the sole purpose of fatiguing them into compliance with his measures.

He has dissolved Representative Houses repeatedly, for opposing with manly firmness his invasions on the rights of the people.

He has refused for a long time, after such dissolutions, to cause others to be elected; whereby the Legislative powers, incapable of Annihilation, have returned to the People at large for their exercise; the State remaining in the mean time exposed to all the dangers of invasion from without, and convulsions within.

He has endeavoured to prevent the population of these States; for that purpose obstructing the Laws for Naturalization of Foreigners; refusing to pass others to encourage their migrations hither, and raising the conditions of new Appropriations of Lands.

He has obstructed the Administration of Justice, by refusing his Assent to Laws for establishing Judiciary powers.

He has made Judges dependent on his Will alone, for the tenure of their offices, and the amount and payment of their salaries.

He has erected a multitude of New Offices, and sent hither swarms of Officers to harrass our people, and eat out their substance.

He has kept among us, in times of peace, Standing Armies without the Consent of our legislatures.

He has affected to render the Military independent of and superior to the Civil power.

He has combined with others to subject us to a jurisdiction foreign to our constitution, and unacknowledged by our laws; giving his Assent to their Acts of pretended Legislation:

For Quartering large bodies of armed troops among us:

For protecting them, by a mock Trial, from punishment for any Murders which they should commit on the Inhabitants of these States:

For cutting off our Trade with all parts of the world:

For imposing Taxes on us without our Consent:

For depriving us in many cases, of the benefits of Trial by Jury:

For transporting us beyond Seas to be tried for pretended offences

For abolishing the free System of English Laws in a neighbouring Province, establishing therein an Arbitrary government, and enlarging its Boundaries so as to render it at once an example and fit instrument for introducing the same absolute rule into these Colonies:

For taking away our Charters, abolishing our most valuable Laws, and altering fundamentally the Forms of our Governments:

For suspending our own Legislatures, and declaring themselves invested with power to legislate for us in all cases whatsoever.

He has abdicated Government here, by declaring us out of his Protection and waging War against us.

He has plundered our seas, ravaged our Coasts, burnt our towns, and destroyed the lives of our people.

He is at this time transporting large Armies of foreign Mercenaries to compleat the works of death, desolation and tyranny, already begun with circumstances of Cruelty & perfidy scarcely paralleled in the most barbarous ages, and totally unworthy the Head of a civilized nation.

He has constrained our fellow Citizens taken Captive on the high Seas to bear Arms against their Country, to become the executioners of their friends and Brethren, or to fall themselves by their Hands.

He has excited domestic insurrections amongst us, and has endeavoured to bring on the inhabitants of our frontiers, the merciless Indian Savages, whose known rule of warfare, is an undistinguished destruction of all ages, sexes and conditions.

In every stage of these Oppressions We have Petitioned for Redress in the most humble terms: Our repeated Petitions have been answered only by repeated injury. A Prince whose character is thus marked by every act which may define a Tyrant, is unfit to be the ruler of a free people.

Nor have We been wanting in attentions to our Brittish brethren. We have warned them from time to time of attempts by their legislature to extend an unwarrantable jurisdiction over us. We have reminded them of the circumstances of our emigration and settlement here.

We have appealed to their native justice and magnanimity, and we have conjured them by the ties of our common kindred to disavow these usurpations, which, would inevitably interrupt our connections and correspondence. They too have been deaf to the voice of justice and of consanguinity. We must, therefore, acquiesce in the necessity, which denounces our Separation, and hold them, as we hold the rest of mankind, Enemies in War, in Peace Friends.

We, therefore, the Representatives of the united States of America, in General Congress, Assembled, appealing to the Supreme Judge of the world for the rectitude of our intentions, do, in the Name, and by Authority of the good People of these Colonies, solemnly publish and declare, That these United Colonies are, and of Right ought to be Free and Independent States; that they are Absolved from all Allegiance to the British Crown, and that all political connection between them and the State of Great Britain, is and ought to be totally dissolved; and that as Free and Independent States, they have full Power to levy War, conclude Peace, contract Alliances, establish Commerce, and to do all other Acts and Things which Independent States may of right do. And for the support of this Declaration, with a firm reliance on the protection of divine Providence, we mutually pledge to each other our Lives, our Fortunes and our sacred Honor.

Georgia

Button Gwinnett
Lyman Hall
George Walton

North Carolina

William Hooper
Joseph Hewes
John Penn

South Carolina

Edward Rutledge
Thomas Heyward, Jr.
Thomas Lynch, Jr.
Arthur Middleton

Massachusetts

John Hancock

Maryland

Samuel Chase
William Paca
Thomas Stone
Charles Carroll of Carrollton

Virginia

George Wythe
Richard Henry Lee
Thomas Jefferson
Benjamin Harrison
Thomas Nelson, Jr.
Francis Lightfoot Lee
Carter Braxton

Pennsylvania

Robert Morris
Benjamin Rush
Benjamin Franklin
John Morton
George Clymer
James Smith
George Taylor
James Wilson
George Ross

Delaware

Caesar Rodney
George Read
Thomas McKean

New York

William Floyd
Philip Livingston
Francis Lewis
Lewis Morris

New Jersey

Richard Stockton
John Witherspoon
Francis Hopkinson
John Hart
Abraham Clark

New Hampshire

Josiah Bartlett
William Whipple

Massachusetts

Samuel Adams
John Adams
Robert Treat Paine
Elbridge Gerry

Rhode Island

Stephen Hopkins
William Ellery

Connecticut

Roger Sherman
Samuel Huntington
William Williams
Oliver Wolcott

New Hampshire

Matthew Thornton

★ A PATRIOT'S HISTORY LESSON ★

Constitution of the United States
March 4, 1789

The Constitution of the United States is the supreme law of the United States of America. We the People ….

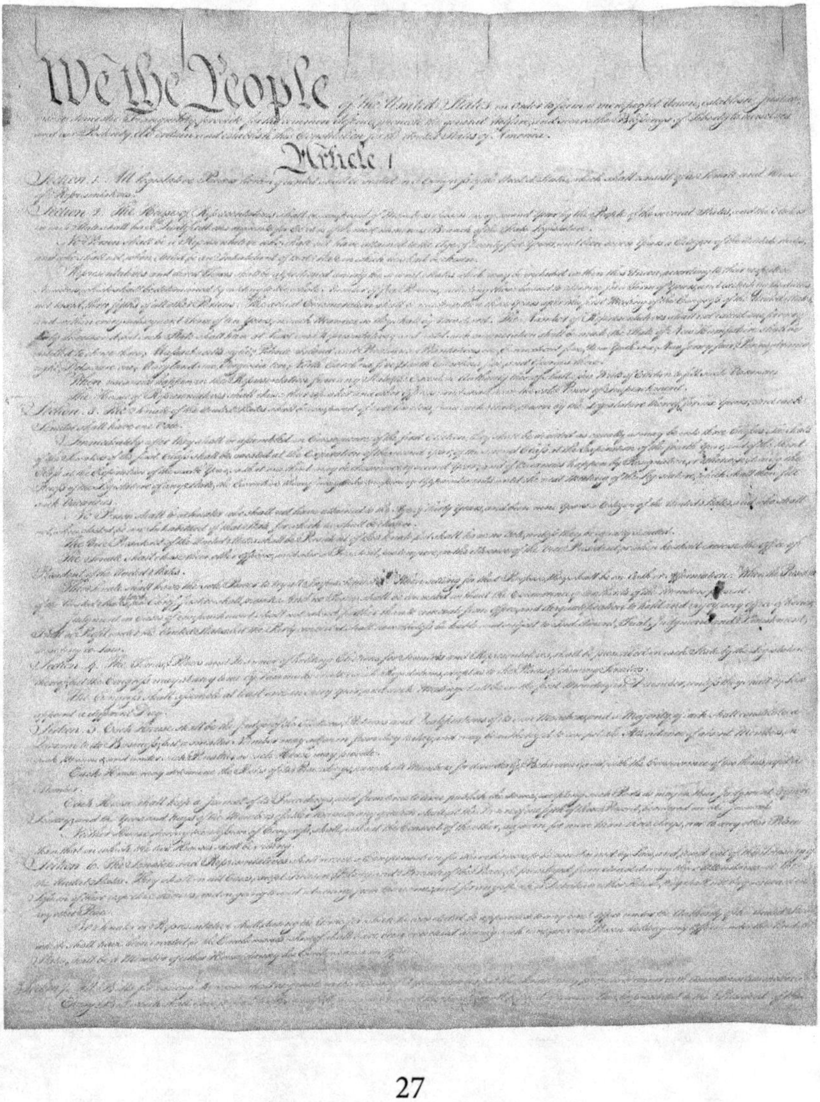
We the People

Article 1

BILL of RIGHTS
December 15, 1791

The United States Bill of Rights comprises the first ten amendments to the United States Constitution. The Bill of Rights amendments add to the Constitution specific guarantees of personal freedoms and rights, clear limitations on the government's power in judicial and other proceedings, and explicit declarations that all powers not specifically granted to the U.S Congress by the Constitution are reserved for the states or the people.

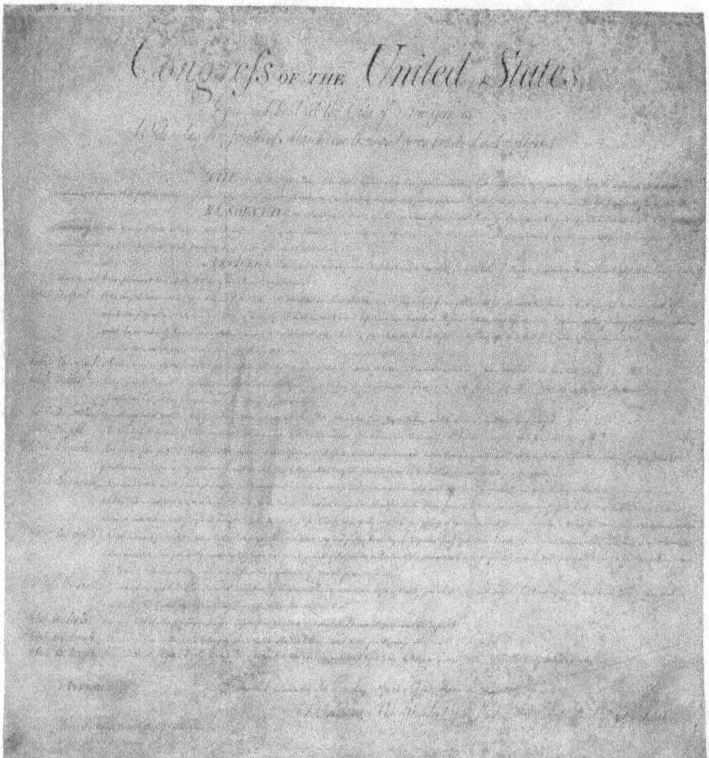
Congress of the United States

First Ten Amendments

Freedom of Religion, Speech, Press, Assembly, and Petition

Right to Keep and Bear Arms

No Quartering of Soldiers

Freedom from Unreasonable Searches and Seizures

Right to Due Process of Law, Freedom from Self-Incrimination

Right to Speedy and Public Trial and Counsel

Right of Trial by Jury

Freedom from Excessive Bail, Cruel and Unusual Punishment

Rights of the People

Rights Reserved to the States

"Ah Liberty" honors those who have been vigilant protectors of Liberty in the past and cries out to the strong and the selfless of today to preserve the Liberty which is the very essence of our American heritage.

- Colonel Clifton P. Schroeder, USMC, Retired

Ah Liberty!

Sweet, Sweet Liberty!
how bitter
was the winter
of your planting!

Sweet seed
sprouted in the blood
of our fathers...
valiant men
with frozen stumps for feet
bleeding in the snow!

What glint of heaven's hope
rekindled freedom's flame
at Valley Forge!
for there, giant men
raised up to smash
the shackles of tyranny forever
to raise and shape
a new and glorious land!

America...
how bitter was the winter
of your planting!
how rich the blood
which nurtured you
through all the years
of sacrifice and building!
And now the Sequoias
of Liberty
thirst... they thirst
need watering again
with grateful tears
of strong and selfless men

Liberty!
sweet, sweet Liberty!
may your lamp
shine bright as a
thousand suns forever!
And may God be praised
for your lamp upraised
may God be praised
for Liberty
Ah...Liberty!

"For Those Who Asked Not And Gave All"

Wendell Schroeder ©1976 text and music

An American Patriot's Book of Quotes

Abraham Lincoln
1809-1865
16th American President

NO. 1

Be sure you put your feet in the right place, THEN STAND FIRM.

- Abraham Lincoln

NO. 2

AMERICA will never be destroyed from outside. If we falter and lose our freedoms, it will be because WE DESTROYED OURSELVES.

- Abraham Lincoln

NO. 3

A HOUSE DIVIDED against itself CANNOT STAND.

I believe this government cannot endure, permanently half slave or half free.

I do not expect the house to fall - I do expect it will cease to be divided. It will become all one thing or the other.

- Abraham Lincoln

NO. 4

Those who **DENY FREEDOM**
to others deserve it not for themselves,
and, under a just God,
CANNOT LONG RETAIN IT.

- Abraham Lincoln

NO. 5

WE ALL DECLARE FOR LIBERTY

But in using the same word we do not all mean the same thing. With some the word LIBERTY may mean for each man to do as he pleases with himself, and the product of his labor; while others, the same word may mean for some men to do as they please with other men, and the product of other men's labor. Here are two, not only different, but incompatible things, called the same name - LIBERTY.

And it follows that each of these things is, by the respective parties, called by two different and incompatible names.. LIBERTY and TYRANNY.

- Abraham Lincoln

NO. 6

I am a firm believer in the people.
If given the truth, they can be depended upon to meet any national crisis.

The point is to bring them the Real Facts!

- Abraham Lincoln

NO. 7

We The People Are the rightful masters of both Congress and the Courts, not to overthrow the Constitution but to overthrow the men who would pervert the Constitution.

- Abraham Lincoln

NO. 8

At what point is the approach of danger to be expected? I answer, if it ever reach us, it must spring up amongst us. If destruction be our lot, we must ourselves be its author and finisher. As a nation of FREE MEN, we must Live Through All Time or Die By Suicide.

- Abraham Lincoln

NO. 9

My concern is not whether God is on my side; My concern is to be on God's side.

- Abraham Lincoln

NO. 10

Any people anywhere,

being inclined and having the power, have the right to rise up, and shake off the existing government, and form a new one that suits them better. This is a most valuable - a most sacred right - a right, which we hope and believe, is to Liberate the World.

- Abraham Lincoln

NO. 11

That Government ..
of the People,
by the People,
for the People,
Shall Not Perish From This Earth.

- Abraham Lincoln

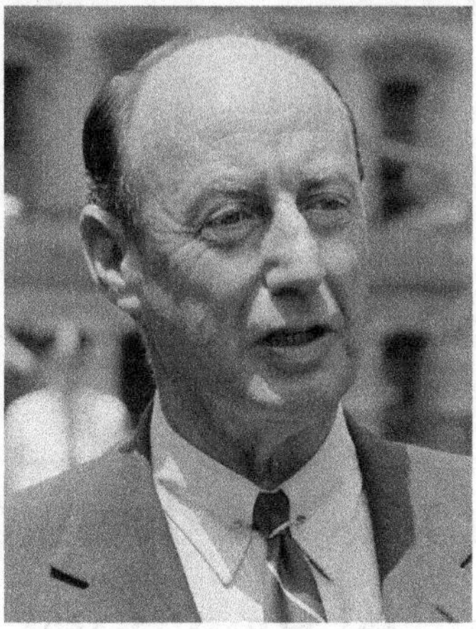

Adlai Stevenson
1900-1965
31st Governor of Illinois (D)

NO. 12

A FREE SOCIETY
is one where it is safe to be unpopular.

- Adlai E. Stevenson

NO.13

Communism is the death of the soul.
It is the organization of total conformity.
In short, TYRANNY !!
AND
It is committed to making
TYRANNY UNIVERSAL.

- Adlai E. Stevenson

Alexander Hamilton
1755-1804
Founding Father of United States

NO. 14

It's not tyranny we desire; it's a just, LIMITED, Federal Government

- Alexander Hamilton

NO. 15

There is a certain enthusiasm in LIBERTY, that makes human nature rise above itself, in acts of BRAVERY AND HEROISM.

- Alexander Hamilton

NO. 16

REAL LIBERTY is neither found in despotism or extremes of democracy, but in moderate governments.

- Alexander Hamilton

NO. 17

The best we can hope for concerning the people at large is that they BE PROPERLY ARMED.

- Alexander Hamilton

NO. 18

Those who stand for nothing FALL FOR ANYTHING.

- Alexander Hamilton

Alexis de Tocqueville
1805-1859
French Diplomat, historian
Author: Democracy in America

NO. 19

DEMOCRACY and SOCIALISM have nothing in common but one word; EQUALITY. But notice the difference: While democracy seeks EQUALITY in LIBERTY, socialism seeks EQUALITY in SERVITUDE.

- Alexis de Tocqueville

Benjamin Franklin
1706-1790
American Founding Father

NO. 20

Any society that will give up a little liberty to gain a little security will Deserve Neither And Lose Both.

- Benjamin Franklin

NO. 21

It is the first responsibility of every
Citizen to Question Authority.

- Benjamin Franklin

NO. 22

When people find that they
can vote themselves money,
That will herald the
End of the Republic.

- Benjamin Franklin

NO. 23

Make yourself sheep and the
WOLVES WILL EAT YOU!!

- Benjamin Franklin

NO. 24

Whoever would overthrow the liberty
of a nation must begin by subduing
THE FREENESS OF SPEECH.

- Benjamin Franklin

NO. 25

Where LIBERTY dwells, THERE IS MY COUNTRY.

- Benjamin Franklin

NO. 26

God grant that not only the LOVE of LIBERTY but a thorough knowledge of the rights of man MAY PERVADE ALL NATIONS of the Earth.

- Benjamin Franklin

NO. 27

FREEDOM of SPEECH is a principal pillar of a free government; When this support is taken away, the Constitution of a free society is dissolved, and TYRANNY is erected on its ruins.

- Benjamin Franklin

Benjamin Rush
1746-1813
American Founding Father

NO. 28

FREEDOM can exist only in the society of knowledge. Without learning, men are incapable of KNOWING THEIR RIGHTS.

- Benjamin Rush

NO. 29

By removing the Bible from the schools
we would be wasting so much time
and money in punishing criminals and
So Little Pains To Prevent Crime.
Take the Bible out of our schools and
there would be an Explosion in Crime.

- Benjamin Rush

Betsy Ross
1752-1836
Sewed/Created the 1st United States Flag

NO. 30

Stars on a field of BLUE; one for each colony; bars of RED, for the blood of sacrifice; on a ground of WHITE for love and peace.

- Betsy Ross

NO. 31

Your country's flag behold!!

And through his tear-dimmed eyes,
he saw the stars and stripes unfold.

- Betsy Ross

Calvin Coolidge
1872-1933
30th American President

NO. 32

PATRIOTISM is easy to understand in America - It means looking out for yourself by looking out for your country.

- Calvin Coolidge

Carl Schurz
1829-1906
American Statesman & Union Army General

NO. 33

My Country, right or wrong: If right, to keep it right: and if wrong, to be set right.

- Carl Schurz

Charles Thomson
1729-1824
Secretary of the Continental Congress
Designer of the Great Seal of the United States

NO. 34

White signifies purity and innocence, Red, hardiness and valor, and Blue, signifies vigilance, PERSEVERANCE & JUSTICE.

- Charles Thomson

NO. 35

Let the WORLD admire the supposed
Wisdom and Valor of our great men.
Perhaps they may adopt the qualities
that have been ascribed to them,
And Thus Good May Be Done.

- Charles Thomson

Clarence Thomas
Associate Justice of the Supreme Court
of the United States

NO. 36

I do think that our FREEDOMS are at RISK.

- Clarence Thomas

NO. 37

I don't think government has a role in telling people how to live their lives. Maybe a minister does, maybe your belief in God does, maybe there's another set of moral codes, but I Don't Think Government Has A Role.

- Clarence Thomas

Daniel Webster
1782-1852
American Statesman

NO. 38

LIBERTY AND UNION, NOW and FOREVER, ONE and INSEPARABLE!!

- Daniel Webster

NO. 39

There is no nation on Earth Powerful enough to accomplish our overthrow.

Our destruction, should it come at all, will be from another quarter. From the inattention of people to the concerns of their government, from their carelessness and negligence.

I fear that they may place too implicit a confidence in their public servants and fail properly to scrutinize their conduct that in this way they may become the instruments of their own undoing.

- Daniel Webster

NO. 40

Let it be borne on the flag under which we rally in every exigency, that we have ONE COUNTRY, ONE CONSTITUTION, ONE DESTINY.

- Daniel Webster

Dennis Prager
Conservative Radio Talk Show Host and Writer

NO. 41

The BIGGER the government The SMALLER the citizen.

- Dennis Prager

Donald J. Trump
45th American President

NO. 42

MAGA

MAKE AMERICA GREAT AGAIN

- Donald J. Trump

NO. 43

ABOVE ALL, we have reasserted
the idea that, in America, the government
answers to the people. Our guiding
light, our North Star, our unwavering
conviction that we are here to serve the
noble everyday citizens of America.
Our allegiance is not to special interests,
corporations, or global entities,
it's to our children, It's to the
AMERICAN CITIZEN !!
This, I hope, will be our greatest legacy;
Together, we put the American people
back in charge of our country.
WE RESTORED SELF-GOVERNMENT.

- Donald J. Trump

NO. 44

No dream is too big.
No challenge is too great.
Nothing we want for our future
is beyond our reach.

- Donald J. Trump

NO. 45

We are, and must always be, a land of hope, of light, and glory to ALL the world. This is the precious inheritance that we must safeguard at every single turn.

- Donald J. Trump

NO. 46

Today's ceremony, however, has very special meaning because today, we are not merely transferring power from one administration to another or from one party to another, but we are transferring power from Washington, D. C. and GIVING IT BACK TO YOU, THE PEOPLE!

- Donald J. Trump
Inauguration Speech 2017

NO. 47

No nation can long survive that loses faith in its values, history, and heroes, for those are the very sources of OUR UNITY AND OUR VITALITY.

- Donald J. Trump

NO. 48

We restored the idea that in America no one is forgotten, because everyone matters, and Everyone Has A Voice.

- Donald J. Trump

NO. 49

As long as the American people hold in their hearts deep and devoted love of country, then there is nothing that this GREAT NATION cannot achieve.

- Donald J. Trump

NO. 50

Only if we forget who we are, and how we got here, could we ever allow political censorship and blacklisting to take place in America. It's not even thinkable. Shutting down free and open debate violates our own values and most ENDURING TRADITIONS.

- Donald J. Trump

NO. 51

We must never forget
that while Americans will always
have our disagreements, we are a nation
of incredible, decent, faithful, and peace
loving citizens who all want our country
to thrive and flourish and be very, very,
successful and good.
We are a truly Magnificent Nation!

- Donald J. Trump

NO. 52

FREEDOM and LIBERTY … We will never let any socialist / marxist movement take that away from us. We will not bend. We will not break.

There is no mountain we cannot climb, there is no summit we cannot reach, there is no challenge we cannot meet, there is no victory we cannot have. As long as we remember that we are strong and proud and mighty Americans with faith in our hearts, grit in our souls and courage in our veins. We are the Americans who make America great again. We had already done it and now we will have to do it again. We will not bend, we will not back down, we will stand proudly for our flag, and we will start talking about our country's greatness again and again. My fellow Americans made America great again and that represents we have just begun. We are one movement, one people, one family, one glorious nation under God. And together we will make America powerful again, We will make America wealthy again. We will make America strong again. We will make America proud again. We will make America safe again.

We will Make America Great Again !!!!

- Donald J. Trump

Dwight D. Eisenhower
1890-1969
34th President of the United States

NO. 53

History does not long entrust the care of **FREEDOM** to the weak or the timid.

- Dwight D. Eisenhower

NO. 54

**IF you want total security go to prison.
There you are feed, clothed,
given medical care and so on . . .
The ONLY thing lacking is
FREEDOM !!!**

- Dwight D. Eisenhower

NO. 55

Here in America

we descended in blood and in spirit
from revolutionists and rebels -
men and women who dared to
dissent from accepted doctrine.
As their heirs, may we never confuse
honest dissent with disloyal subversion.

- Dwight D. Eisenhower

Frederick Douglas
1818-1895
Abolishionist & Statesman

NO. 56

I am a REPUBLICAN, a black, dyed in the wool Republican, and I never intend to belong to any other party than the PARTY of FREEDOM and PROGRESS !!

- Frederick Douglas

NO. 57

The LIFE of the Nation is secure
only while the Nation is
Honest, Truthful, and Virtuous.

- Frederick Douglas

NO. 58

To supress FREE SPEECH
is a double wrong. It violates the rights
of the hearer as well as those
of the speaker.

- Frederick Douglas

NO. 59

Find out just what any people will quietly submit to and you have the exact measure of injustice and wrong which will be imposed on them.

- Frederick Douglas

NO. 60

I prefer to be true to myself, even at the hazard of insuring the ridicule of others, rather than to be false, and to incur my own abhorrence.

- Frederick Douglas

NO. 61

The thing worse than rebellion is the THING THAT CAUSES REBELLION.

- Frederick Douglas

NO. 62

The Limits of Tyrants are prescribed by the endurance of those whom they oppress.

- Frederick Douglas

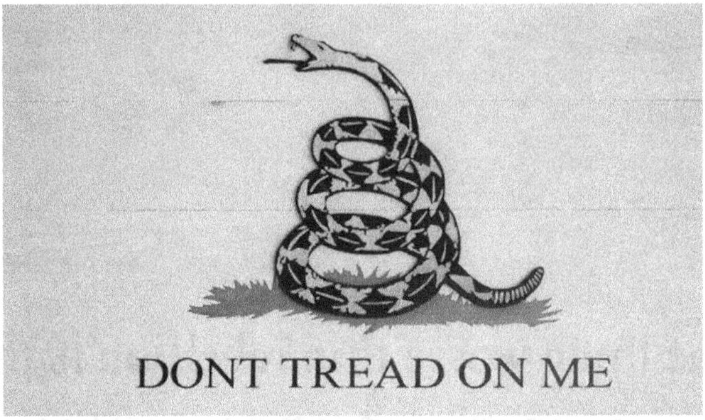

NO. 63

The Gadsden Flag

The Gadsden Flag is an American historical flag with a yellow field depicting a rattlesnake coiled and ready to strike. Below the snake is the legend:

"DONT TREAD ON ME"

The flag was designed in 1775
by the American General and Statesman
Christopher Gadsden.

George Mason
1725-1792
Father of the Bill of Rights

NO. 64

The Freedom of the Press is one of the great bulwarks of LIBERTY.

- George Mason

NO. 65

To DISARM the people is the most effectual way to ENSLAVE them.

- George Mason

NO. 66

There is a passion natural to the mind of man, especially a FREE MAN, which Renders Him Impatient Of Restraint.

- George Mason

George Washington
1732-1799
1st American President

NO. 67

The time is near at hand which must determine whether Americans are to be FREE MEN OR SLAVES.

- George Washington

NO. 68

A FREE PEOPLE ought not only to be armed and disciplined, but they should have sufficient arms and ammunition to maintain a status of **INDEPENDENCE** from any who might attempt to abuse them, which would include their own government.

- George Washington

NO 69

When a government takes away citizens' Right To Bear Arms it becomes the citizens' duty to take away governments right to govern.

- George Washington

NO. 70

The marvel of all history is the patience with which men and women submit to the burdens unnecessarily laid upon them by their governments.

- George Washington

NO. 71

IF the FREEDOM of SPEECH
is taken away then dumb
and silent we may be led,
like sheep, to the slaughter.

- George Washington

NO. 72

FIREARMS are second only to the
Constitution in importance;
they are the peoples'
LIBERTY TEETH.

- George Washington

NO. 73

The very atmosphere of firearms
anywhere restrains evil interference -
they deserve a place of honor
with all that's good.
There is nothing so like to produce
peace as to be well prepared
to meet an enemy.

- George Washington

NO. 74

Guard against the impostures
OF PRETENDED PATRIOTISM.

- George Washington

NO. 75

"DEEDS NOT WORDS"

- George Washington

NO. 76

GOVERNMENT is not reason,
it is not eloquent: it is force.
Like fire, it is a dangerous servant
and a FEARFUL MASTER.

- George Washington

NO.77

The Constitution is the guide
WHICH I NEVER WILL ABANDON.

- George Washington

NO.78

LIBERTY, when it begins to take root, is a plant of rapid growth.

- George Washington

NO. 79

Associate with men of good quality if you esteem your own reputation; for it is better to be alone than in bad company.

- George Washington

James Madison
1751-1836
4th American President

NO. 80

Oppressors can tyrannize only when they achieve a standing army, and enslaved press, and a DISARMED POPULACE.

- James Madison

NO. 81

The truth is that ALL men having power ought to be mistrusted.

\- James Madison

NO. 82

The advancement and diffusion of knowledge is the only guardian of TRUE LIBERTY.

\- James Madison

NO. 83

A WELL REGULATED MILITIA,
being necessary to the Security of a
Free State, the Right of the People
to Keep and Bear Arms
SHALL NOT BE INFRINGED.

- James Madison

NO. 84

The powers delegated by the proposed Constitution to the Federal Government are few and defined.

Those which are to remain in the State Governments are numerous and indefinite.

The former will be exercised principally on external objects, as war, peace, negotiation and foreign commerce. The powers reserved to the several States will extend to all objects which in the ordinary course of affairs, concern the lives and liberties, and properties of the people, and the internal order, improvement and prosperity of the State.

- James Madison

NO. 85

Americans have the right and advantage of being armed - unlike the citizens of the other countries whose governments are afraid to Trust The People With Arms.

- James Madison

NO. 86

The essence of government is power: and power, lodged as it must in human hands, WILL EVER BE LIABLE TO ABUSE.

- James Madison

James Monroe
1758-1831
5th President of the United States

NO. 87

Of the LIBERTY of CONSCIENCE in matters of religious faith, of speech, and of the press; of the trial by jury of the vicinage in civil and criminal cases; of the benefit of the writ of habeas corpus; of the right to keep and bear arms .. If these rights are well defined, and secured against encroachment, it is impossible that government should ever degenerate into tyranny.

\- James Monroe

NO. 88

If it was wise, manly, and patriotic
for us to establish a free government,
it is equally wise to attend
to the necessary means of
its PRESERVATION.

- James Monroe

NO. 89

We must support our rights or lose our
character, and with it, perhaps,
our LIBERTIES.

- James Monroe

John Adams
1735-1826
2nd American President

NO. 90

The decree is gone forth, and it cannot be recalled, that a more equal liberty than has prevailed in other parts of the Earth, must be established in America.

- John Adams

NO. 91

There is danger from ALL men,
the only maxim of a free government
ought to be to trust no man living with
power to endanger the public liberty.

- John Adams

NO. 92

Our Constitution was made only
for a moral and religious people.
It is wholly inadequate to the
government of any other.

- John Adams

NO. 93

You will never know how much
it has cost my generation to
PRESERVE YOUR FREEDOM.
I hope you will make good use of it.

- John Adams

NO. 94

ARMS in the hands of the citizens
may be used at individual discretion
for the defense of the country,
the overthrow of tyranny
or private self defense.

- John Adams

John Jay
1745-1829
United States Founding Father / Patriot

NO. 95

Among the many objects to which a wise and free people find it necessary to direct their attention, that of providing for their SAFETY seems to be first.

- John Jay

NO. 96

To contend for or own liberty,
and to deny that blessing to others,
involves an inconsistency
NOT TO BE EXCUSED.

- John Jay

John F. Kennedy
1917-1963
35th American President

NO. 97

Liberty without Learning is always in peril and Learning without Liberty is always in vain.

- John F. Kennedy

NO. 98

Let every nation know, whether it
wishes us well or ill, that we shall pay
any price, bear any burden, meet any
hardship, support any friend,
oppose any foe to assure the
Survival and the Success of LIBERTY.

- John F. Kennedy

NO. 99

And so my fellow Americans; ask not what your country can do for you, ask what you can do for your country. My fellow citizens of the world; ask not what America will do for you, but what together we can do for the **FREEDOM OF MAN.**

- John F. Kennedy

John Wayne
1907-1979
American Film Actor

NO. 100

ALL I'M FOR is the LIBERTY of the INDIVIDUAL.

- John Wayne

NO. 101

When I was a sophomore at USC,
I was a socialist, pretty much to the left.
But when I left the university, I got wise.
I'd read about what had happened to
Russia in 1917 when the
COMMUNISTS TOOK OVER.

- John Wayne

NO. 102

Sure I wave the American flag.
Do you know a better flag to wave?
Sure, I love my country
with all her faults.
I am not ashamed of that,
NEVER HAVE BEEN,
NEVER WILL BE.

- John Wayne

Kristi Noem
Governor of South Dakota

NO. 103

Under God, the People Rule.

- Kristi Noem

NO. 104

We have inherited the greatest legacy of freedom in human history. We Have To Fight To Hold On To It!

- Kristi Noem

NO. 105

We need an energy plan that prioritizes American Energy and American Families.

- Kristi Noem

NO. 106

No Mandates. No Lockdowns.
Just FREEDOM
and PERSONAL LIBERTY
- That's the South Dakota way.

- Kristi Noem

NO. 107

In South Dakota,
we will protect FREEDOM
and we will not allow it to go extinct.

- Kristi Noem

NO. 108

LESS GOVERNMENT. MORE FREEDOM!

- Kristi Noem

Lee Greenwood
Country Music Artist

NO. 109

"And I'm proud to be an American,
where at least I know I'm free.
And I won't forget the men who died,
who gave that right to me."

- Lee Greenwood

Mark Levin
American Patriot

NO. 110

There are people who are trying to take advantage of this country and destroy it. If We Don't Stand Up Against It, nobody is going to stand up against it.

- Mark Levin

NO. 111

What the Founding Fathers created in the
Constitution is the most magnificent
government on the face of the Earth,
and the reason is this: because
it was intended to preserve the
American Society and
the American Spirit,
Not To Transform It Or Destroy It.

- Mark Levin

NO. 112

Totalitarian propaganda can outrageously insult common sense only where common sense has lost its validity.

- Mark Levin

NO. 113

We should remember that the Declaration of Independence is not merely a historical document. It is an explicit recognition that our rights derive not from the King of England, not from the judiciary, not from government at all, but from God.

- Mark Levin

NO. 114

In Short, Marx understood the power of mass communication and the need to control it and shape it to frame the events and opinions. In Other Words, the purpose was to PROPAGANDIZE, NOT INFORM.

- Mark Levin

NO. 115

Of course, the primary difference between the counterrevolution and the American Revolution is that the former seeks to destroy American society and impose autocratic rule, and the latter sought to protect American society and institute representative government.

- Mark Levin

NO. 116

Conservatism is the antidote to tyranny. It's the only one. It's based on thousands of years of human experience. There is nothing narrow about the conservative philosophy. It is a magnificent philosophy for the ages, for all times.

- Mark Levin

NO. 117

The Founders believed, and the Conservative agrees, in the dignity of the individual; that we, as human beings, have a right to live, live freely, and pursue that which motivates us not because man or some government says so, but because these are God-Given Natural Rights.

- Mark Levin

Mark Twain
1835-1910
American Author & Humorist

NO. 118

PATRIOTISM is supporting your country ALL of the time, and your government WHEN it deserves it.

- Mark Twain

NO. 119

Each man must himself alone decide what is right and what is wrong, which course is patriotic and which isn't.

You cannot shirk this and be a man.

To decide against your conviction is to be an unqualified and excusable traitor, both to yourself and to your country.

Let men label you as they may.

- Mark Twain

Martin Luther King Jr.
1929-1968
American Civil Rights Leader

NO. 120

I have a dream that one day
my little four children will one day live
in a nation where they will not be judged
by the color of their skin but by the
CONTENT OF THEIR CHARACTER.

- Martin Luther King Jr.
August 28th, 1963

NO. 121

WE may ALL have come on different ships, but we are in the same boat now.

- Martin Luther King Jr.

NO. 122

The ultimate measure of a man is not where he stands in moments of comfort and convenience, but where he stands at Times Of Challenge And Controversy.

- Martin Luther King Jr.

Milton Friedman
1912-2006
American Economist

NO. 123

A society that puts equality before freedom will get neither. A society that puts Freedom Before Equality will get a high degree of both.

- Milton Friedman

NO. 124

Government can raise taxes
because it can persuade a
sizable fraction of the populace
THAT SOMEBODY ELSE WILL PAY.

- Milton Friedman

Nathan Hale
1755-1776
American Patriot

NO. 125

I only regret that I have but one life to lose FOR MY COUNTRY.

- Nathan Hale

Newt Gingrich
American Politician, College Professor,
Historian & Author

NO. 126

I believe we are in a struggle over whether or not we are going to Save America!!

- Newt Gingrich

NO. 127

We're at the crossroads. Down one road is a European centralized bureaucratic socialist welfare system in which politicians and bureaucrats define the future. Down the other road is a proud, solid, reaffirmation of AMERICAN EXCEPTIONALISM.

- Newt Gingrich

Noah Webster
1758-1843
Father of American Education

NO. 128

IF the citizens neglect their Duty and place unprincipled men in office . . . Corrupt or incompetent men will be appointed to execute the laws; the public revenues will be squandered on unworthy men; and the rights of the citizens will be Violated And Disregarded.

- Noah Webster

Patrick Henry
1736-1799
Governor of Virginia

NO. 129

GIVE ME LIBERTY
or
GIVE ME DEATH !!

- Patrick Henry

NO. 130

When the American Spirit
was in it's youth,
The language of America was different;
LIBERTY, Sir, was the primary object.

- Patrick Henry

NO. 131

The great object is that
EVERY MAN BE ARMED.

- Patrick Henry

NO. 132

Guard With Jealous Attention
the Public Liberty. Suspect everyone
who approaches that jewel. Unfortunately,
nothing will preserve it but downright
force. Whenever you give up
that force you are ruined.

- Patrick Henry

NO. 133

The LIBERTIES of a people never
were, nor ever will be, secure,
when the transactions of their rulers
may be canceled from them.

- Patrick Henry

NO. 134

We are not weak if we make proper use of those means which the God of Nature has placed in our power.. the battle, Sir, is not to the strong alone it is to the Vigilant, the Active, the Brave.

- Patrick Henry

NO. 135

Perfect Freedom is as necessary to the health and vigor of commerce as it is to the Health and Vigor of Citizenship.

- Patrick Henry

NO. 136

Gentleman may cry,
PEACE, PEACE . . . but there is no peace.

The war is actually begun! The next gale that sweeps from the north will bring to our ears the clash of resounding arms! Our brethren are already in the field! Why stand we here idle? What is it gentlemen wish? What would they have? Is life so dear, or peace so sweet, as to be purchased at the price of chains and slavery?? Forbid it, Almighty God!

I know not what course others may take; but as for me..

"Give me Liberty or Give me Death!!"

- Patrick Henry

NO. 137

IF this be TREASON ..
make the most of it !!

- Patrick Henry

Ralph Waldo Emerson
1803-1882
American Philosopher, Lecturer,
Essayist & Poet

NO. 138

America is another name for opportunity.
Our whole history appears like a
last effort of DIVINE PROVIDENCE
on behalf of the human race.

- Ralph Waldo Emerson

Robert Frost
1874-1963
American Poet

NO. 138

You have FREEDOM when you're easy in your saddle.

- Robert Frost

Robert J. McCracken
1904-1973
Clergyman

NO. 140

We on this continent should never forget that men first crossed the Atlantic not to find soil for their ploughs but to secure LIBERTY FOR THEIR SOULS.

- Robert J. McCracken

Ron DeSantis
Governor of Florida

NO. 141

WE NEED TO SAVE AMERICA!!

- Ron DeSantis

NO. 142

If you look at Washington DC right now, we do not have a system that the Founding Fathers envisioned, where people go to Washington and be part of the servant class. Instead, we have a permanent political class that fashions itself the rulers of the people.

- Ron DeSantis

NO. 143

Very rarely do firearms restrictions affect criminals. They really only affect LAW-ABIDING CITIZENS.

- Ron DeSantis

NO. 144

We must enforce the laws we have on the books, secure our borders, and deny special benefits to illegal immigrants such as in-state tuition rates. This approach is best for American citizens and is fair to those who have taken the time and effort to go through THE LEGAL IMMIGRATION PROCESS.

- Ron DeSantis

Ronald Reagan
1911-2004
40th American President

NO. 145

FREEDOM is never more than one generation away from extinction. We didn't pass it to our children in the bloodstream. It must be fought for, protected, and handed on for them to do the same.

\- Ronald Reagan

NO. 146

America must remain
freedom's staunchest friend,
for FREEDOM is our best ally.
AND IT IS THE WORLD'S
ONLY HOPE.

- Ronald Reagan

NO. 147

Concentrated power has always been the ENEMY OF LIBERTY.

- Ronald Reagan

NO. 148

Man is not free unless GOVERNMENT IS LIMITED.

- Ronald Reagan

NO. 149

I have seen the rise of fascism and communism. Both philosophies glorify the arbitrary power of the state. But both theories fail. Both deny those GOD GIVEN LIBERTIES that are the inalienable right of each person on this planet, indeed, they deny the existence of God.

- Ronald Reagan

NO. 150

I didn't leave the Democratic Party.
THE PARTY LEFT ME !!

- Ronald Reagan

NO. 151

If we ever forget that we are
ONE NATION UNDER GOD,
Then we will be a nation gone under.

- Ronald Reagan

NO. 152

The most terrifying words in
the English language are:
I'm from the government
and I'm here to help!

- Ronald Reagan

NO. 153

Government's first duty
is to protect the people,
NOT RUN THEIR LIVES.

- Ronald Reagan

NO. 154

How do you tell a communist?
Well, it's someone who reads
Marx and Lenin.
And how do you tell an anti-communist?
It's someone who understands
Marx and Lenin.

- Ronald Reagan

NO. 155

It was LEADERSHIP here at home that gave us strong American influence abroad, and the collapse of Imperial Communism. Great nations have responsibilities to lead, and we should always be cautious of those who would lower our profile, because they might just wind up lowering our flag.

- Ronald Reagan

NO. 156

I've always believed that this blessed land was set apart in a special way, that some divine plan placed this great continent here between the oceans to be found by people from every corner of the Earth who had a special love for freedom and the courage to uproot themselves, leave homeland and friends, to come to a strange land. And coming here they created something new in all the history of mankind - a land where man is not beholden to government,

Government Is Beholden To Man.

- Ronald Reagan

Samuel Adams
1722-1803
American Patriot and Statesman

NO. 157

It is the interest of tyrants to reduce the people to ignorance and vice. For they cannot live in any country where VIRTUE AND KNOWLEDGE PREVAIL.

- Samual Adams

NO. 158

If ye love wealth greater than liberty, the tranquility of servitude better than the animating contest for freedom, go home from us in peace. We ask not your counsels or your arms. Crouch down and lick the hands which feed you, and may posterity forget that ye were our countrymen.

- Samual Adams

NO. 159

We have proclaimed to the world
our determination to die **FREE MEN**,
rather than to live as slaves.

- Samual Adams

NO. 160

If ever a time should come,
when vain and aspiring men
shall possess the highest seats
in Government, our country will
stand in need of its experienced
PATRIOTS TO PREVENT ITS RUIN.

- Samual Adams

Theodore Roosevelt
1858-1919
26th American President

NO. 161

To sit home, read ones favorite paper, and scoff at the misdeeds of the men who do things is easy, but it is markedly ineffective. It is what evil men count upon the good men's doing.

- Theodore Roosevelt

NO. 162

A soft, easy life is not worth living,
if it impairs the fibre of brain and heart
and muscle. We must dare to be great;
and we must realize greatness is the fruit
of toil and sacrifice and high courage
For us is the life of action, of strenuous
performance of duty; let us live in the
harness, striving mightily;
let us rather run the risk of
Wearing Out Than Rusting Out.

- Theodore Roosevelt

NO. 163

We must show, not merely in great crisis, but in the everyday affairs of life, the qualities of practical intelligence, of courage, of hardihood, and endurance, and above all the power of devotion to a lofty ideal, which made great the men who founded this Republic in the days of Washington, which made great the men who preserved this Republic in the days of Abraham Lincoln.

\- Theodore Roosevelt

NO. 164

THE MAN IN THE ARENA

It is not the critic who counts; not the man who points out how the strong man stumbles, or where the doer of deeds could have done them better. The credit belongs to the man who is actually in the arena, whose face is marred by dust and sweat and blood; who strives valiantly; who errs, who comes short again and again, because there is no effort without error and shortcomings; but who does actually strive to do the deeds; who knows great enthusiasms, the great devotions; who spends himself in a worthy cause; who at the best knows in the end the triumph of high achievement, and who at the worst, if he fails, at least fails while daring greatly, so that his place shall never be with those cold and timid souls who neither know victory nor defeat.

- Theodore Roosevelt
April 23, 1910

Thomas Jefferson
1743-1826
3rd American President
Founding Father

NO. 165

All TYRANNY needs to gain a foothold is for the people of good conscience to remain silent.

- Thomas Jefferson

NO. 166

What country can preserve its liberties if the rulers are not warned from time to time that their people preserve the spirit of resistance?

Let them take arms !!

- Thomas Jefferson

NO. 167

Laws that forbid the carrying of arms, disarm only those who are neither inclined nor determined to commit crimes.

- Thomas Jefferson

NO. 168

Evil triumphs when
Good men do nothing.

- Thomas Jefferson

NO. 169

The price of FREEDOM
is eternal vigilance.

- Thomas Jefferson

NO. 170

The government is the servant
NOT the Master of the People.

- Thomas Jefferson

NO. 171

When all government, domestic and foreign, in little as in great things, shall be drawn to Washington as the center of all power, it will become as venal and oppressive as the government from which we separated.

- Thomas Jefferson

NO. 172

Most BAD government has grown out of too much government.

- Thomas Jefferson

NO. 173

When governments fear the people
there is LIBERTY.
When the people fear the government
there is TYRANNY.

\- Thomas Jefferson

NO. 174

TYRANNY is defined as that which
is legal for the government
but illegal for the citizenry.

\- Thomas Jefferson

NO. 175

Experience has shown, that even under the best forms of government those entrusted with power, in time, and by slow operations, perverted it into TYRANNY.

- Thomas Jefferson

NO. 176

My God! How little do my countrymen know what precious blessings they are in possession of, and which no other people on Earth enjoy!

- Thomas Jefferson

NO. 177

The people are the only sure reliance for the preservation of our LIBERTY.

- Thomas Jefferson

NO. 178

No free man shall ever be barred the use of ARMS.

- Thomas Jefferson

NO. 179

Single act of tyranny may be ascribed to the accidental opinion of the day; but a series of oppressions, begun at a distinguished period, and pursued unalterably through every change of administration too plainly proves a deliberate, systemic plan of REDUCING US TO SLAVERY.

- Thomas Jefferson

NO. 180

One loves to possess ARMS
though they hope never to
have the occasion for them.

- Thomas Jefferson

NO. 181

It is error alone which needs
the support of government.
Truth Can Stand On Its Own.

- Thomas Jefferson

NO. 182

The natural progress of things is for **LIBERTY** to yield and the government to gain ground.

- Thomas Jefferson

NO. 183

No government ought to be without censors; and where the **PRESS IS FREE** no one ever will.

- Thomas Jefferson

NO. 184

Yes, we did produce a near perfect Republic. But will they keep it? Or will they, in the enjoyment of plenty, lose the memory of freedom? Material abundance without character IS THE PATH TO DESTRUCTION.

- Thomas Jefferson

NO. 185

The TREE of LIBERTY must be refreshed from time to time with the Blood Of Patriots And Tyrants.

- Thomas Jefferson

NO. 186

THE SPIRIT OF RESISTANCE
to government is so valuable on certain occasions, that I wish it to be always kept alive. It will often be exercised at all.
I like a little rebellion now and then!!

- Thomas Jefferson

NO. 187

I would rather be exposed to the inconveniences of too much LIBERTY than to those attending too small a degree of it.

- Thomas Jefferson

NO. 188

A strong body makes the mind strong. As to the species of exercises, I advise the gun. While this gives moderate exercise to the body, it gives boldness, enterprise and independence to the mind. Games played with the ball, and others of the nature, are too violent for the body and stamp no character on the mind. Let Your Gun Therefore Be Your Constant Companion Of Your Walks.

- Thomas Jefferson

NO. 189

The price of freedom is ETERNAL VIGILANCE.

- Thomas Jefferson

NO. 190

EVERY CITIZEN should be a soldier. This was the case with the Greeks and Romans, and must be that of every free state.

- Thomas Jefferson

NO. 191

RIGHTFUL LIBERTY
is unobstructed action according to
our will within limits drawn around
us by the equal rights of others. I do
not add "within the limits of the law"
because law is often but the Tyrants' will,
and always so when it violates
THE RIGHTS OF THE INDIVIDUAL.

- Thomas Jefferson

Thomas Paine
1737-1809
Founding Father of America

NO. 192

ARMS discourage and keep the invader and plunderer in awe, and preserve order in the world as well as property.

- Thomas Paine

NO. 193

Government, even in its best state, is but a Necessary Evil; in its worst state, an Intolerable One.

- Thomas Paine

NO. 194

An Army of Principles can penetrate where an Army of Soldiers cannot.

- Thomas Paine

NO. 195

LEAD, FOLLOW …

or get out of the way!!!

- Thomas Paine

NO. 196

The duty of a TRUE PATRIOT

is to protect his country

from his government.

- Thomas Paine

NO. 197

If there must be trouble,
let it be in my day,
That My Child May Have Peace.

- Thomas Paine

NO. 198

Those who expect to reap the Blessings
of Freedom, must like men, undergo
THE FATIGUE OF SUPPORTING IT.

- Thomas Paine

NO. 199

TYRANNY, like hell, is not easily conquered; yet we have this consolation with us, that the harder the conflict, the more glorious the triumph.

- Thomas Paine

NO. 200

He that would make his own LIBERTY secure must guard even his enemy from oppression; for if he violates this duty he establishes a precedent that will reach to himself.

- Thomas Paine

NO. 201

These are the times that try men's souls.

The summer soldier and the sunshine patriot will, in the crisis, shrink from the service of their country; but he that stands it now, deserves the love and thanks of man and woman.

- Thomas Paine

Thomas Sowell
American Economist & Senior Fellow
at Hoover Institute

NO. 202

If you are not prepared to use force to defend civilization, then be Prepared To Accept Barbarism.

- Thomas Sowell

NO. 203

Socialism in general has a record of failure so blatant that only an Intellectual Could Ignore Or Evade It.

- Thomas Sowell

NO. 204

The most basic question is not what is best, But Who Shall Decide What Is Best.

- Thomas Sowell

NO. 205

AS HISTORY HAS SHOWN,
especially in the twentieth century,
one of the first things an ideologue
will do after achieving
absolute power is KILL!!

- Thomas Sowell

NO. 206

FREEDOM has cost too much blood
and glory to be relinquished at the
Cheap Price Of Rhetoric.

- Thomas Sowell

NO. 207

Since this is an era when many people are concerned about "fairness" and "social justice" What is your "fair share" of what someone else has worked for?

- Thomas Sowell

NO. 208

Much of the social history of the Western World over the past three decades has involved replacing what worked with what sounded good.

- Thomas Sowell

NO. 209

The next time some academic tells you how important diversity is, ask how many Republicans / Conservatives there are in their sociology department.

- Thomas Sowell

Ulysses S. Grant
1822-1885
18th American President & Union Army General

NO. 210

GOD gave us LINCOLN & LIBERTY, let us fight for both.

- Ulysses S. Grant

NO. 211

Our GREAT REPUBLIC,
may those who seek the blessings
of its institutions and protection
of its flag remember the
obligations they impose.

- Ulysses S. Grant

NO. 212

In every battle there comes a time when
both sides consider themselves beaten,
then he who continues the attack wins.

- Ulysses S. Grant

NO. 213

If we are to have another contest in the
near future of our national existence,
I predict that the dividing line will not
be Mason and Dixon but between
PATRIOTISM and INTELLIGENCE
on one side, and Superstition,
Ambition and Ignorance on the other.

- Ulysses S. Grant

NO. 214

The right of the revolution is an inherent one. When people are oppressed by their government, it is the natural right they enjoy to relieve themselves of oppression, if they are strong enough, whether by withdrawal from it, or by overthrowing it and substituting a government more acceptable.

- Ulysses S. Grant

NO. 215

Let us labor for the security of free thought, free speech, pure morals, unfettered religious sentiments, and equal rights and privileges for ALL MEN, irrespective of Nationality, Color, or Religion.

- Ulysses S. Grant

NO. 216

FREEDOM is NEVER FREE !!

- Unknown

NO. 217

When government is big enough
to provide you everything,
it is big enough to take everything.

- Unknown

NO. 218

LIBERTY with DANGER
to
PEACE with SLAVERY !!

- Unknown

NO. 219

The ultimate minority
is the INDIVIDUAL.

- Unknown

NO. 220

INDIVIDUAL LIBERTY and the FREEDOM of the AMERICAN CITIZEN shall be considered in ALL matters of government.

- Unknown

R. Blake Wilson

R. Blake Wilson was born and raised in Springfield, Illinois in the shadow of Abraham Lincoln. He believes in the American Dream and the Pursuit of Happiness and has lived his life chasing both. His life story is emblematic of an America where the individual is free to fail, succeed, fail and succeed again and again. The quotes in *JOIN, or DIE.* are a reminder to Americans that as long as we live in a United States of America where Individual Liberty and Freedom prevail over Tyranny, future generations of Americans will too … Live the American Dream !! United We Stand, Divided We Fall !!

"JOIN or DIE. An American Patriot's Book of Quotes" is his way of standing up for LIBERTY and FREEDOM in America.

May God Bless America !!!

CPSIA information can be obtained
at www.ICGtesting.com
Printed in the USA
JSHW080039010623
42460JS00002B/11

9 780983 140634